D1606908

APEX PREDATORS
of the Amazon Rain Forest

Harpy Eagle

by Ellen Lawrence

Consultant:

Erin Katz
Director of Community Engagement
The Peregrine Fund
Boise, Idaho

BEARPORT
PUBLISHING

New York, New York

Credits

Cover, © MarcusVDT/Shutterstock, © Dr Morley Read/Shutterstock, and © Chepe Nicoli/Shutterstock; 4, © Thomas Marent/ Minden Pictures/FLPA; 5, © Nick Garbutt/Alamy; 6R, © Cosmographics; 6B, © Ondrej Prosicky/Shutterstock; 7, © Kuttig – Travel – 2/Alamy; 7L, © MarcusVDT/Shutterstock; 8T, © David Tipling/FLPA; 8B, © Laura Duellman/Shutterstock; 9, © MarcusVDT/ Shutterstock; 10, © Mark Wardle/Alamy; 11, © ZSSD/Minden Pictures/FLPA; 12T, © Kokhanchikov/Shutterstock; 12B, © Nick Garbutt/Nature Picture Library; 13BL, © Seaphotoart/Shutterstock; 13R, © Ariadne Van Zandbergen/FLPA; 14, © Pete Oxford/ Minden Pictures/FLPA; 15, © blickwinkel/Alamy; 16, © The Peregrine Fund; 17, © Jeff Cremer; 18, © Pete Oxford/Minden Pictures/ FLPA; 19, © Tui De Roy/Minden Pictures/FLPA; 20, © Tui De Roy/Minden Pictures/FLPA; 21, © Pete Oxford/Minden Pictures/FLPA; 22, © Benson HE/Shutterstock, © MassDream Studio/Shutterstock, © rangizzz/Shutterstock, and © Chepe Nicoli/Shutterstock; 23TL, Public Domain; 23TC, © Travel Stock/Shutterstock; 23TR, © Amit Tekwani/Shutterstock; 23BL, © Dr. Morley Read/ Shutterstock; 23BC, © Lu Lovelock/Shutterstock; 23BR, © critterbiz/Shutterstock.

Publisher: Kenn Goin
Senior Editor: Joyce Tavolacci
Creative Director: Spencer Brinker
Photo Researcher: Ruby Tuesday Books Ltd

Library of Congress Cataloging-in-Publication Data

Names: Lawrence, Ellen, 1967– author.
Title: Harpy eagle / by Ellen Lawrence.
Description: New York, New York : Bearport Publishing Company, Inc., [2017] |
    Series: Apex predators of the amazon rain forest | Audience: Ages 5–8. |
    Includes bibliographical references and index.
Identifiers: LCCN 2016042362 (print) | LCCN 2016051593 (ebook) | ISBN
    9781684020294 (library) | ISBN 9781684020812 (ebook)
Subjects: LCSH: Harpy eagle—Juvenile literature. | Eagles—Juvenile
    literature.
Classification: LCC QL696.F32 L367 2017 (print) | LCC QL696.F32 (ebook) | DDC
    598.9/42—dc23
LC record available at https://lccn.loc.gov/2016042362

For more information, write to Bearport Publishing Company, Inc., 45 West 21st Street, Suite 3B, New York, New York 10010. Printed in the United States of America.

10 9 8 7 6 5 4 3 2 1

Contents

Huge Hunter

There's a rustling sound in a tall tree in the Amazon **rain forest**.

A large monkey is climbing from branch to branch.

Suddenly, there's a flash of white and black feathers.

A huge harpy eagle snatches the monkey with its huge claws.

Then the giant bird carries its **prey** to a high branch and begins to feed.

howler monkey

harpy eagle

Eagles are known as birds of prey. They are also called **raptors**. The word *raptor* means "to grab" or "take by force."

A Harpy Eagle's Home

Harpy eagles live in parts of Central and South America.

They make their homes in thick rain forests, such as the Amazon.

The Amazon is filled with tall trees and thousands of other types of plants.

The harpy eagle shares the forest with many animals, including jaguars, parrots, and millions of insects.

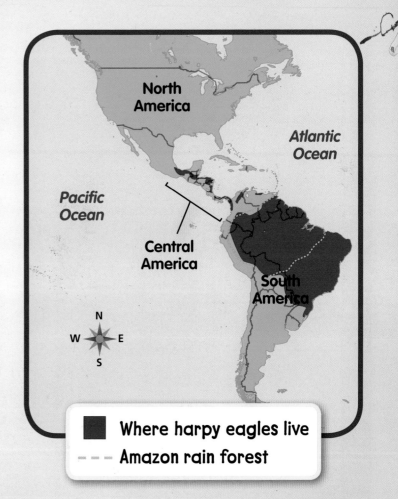

North America

Atlantic Ocean

Pacific Ocean

Central America

South America

N
W E
S

Where harpy eagles live

- - - Amazon rain forest

Harpy eagles like to perch, or rest, in tall trees, such as kapok trees. A kapok tree can grow taller than a 15-story building!

harpy eagle

kapok tree

Supersized Bird

A harpy eagle is one of the largest birds of prey.

It's more than 3 feet (0.9 m) tall, and its wings span 6 feet (1.8 m).

Each of the bird's powerful legs is as thick as a broom handle.

It has four sharp **talons**, or claws, on each foot.

The harpy's back talons can be as long as a grizzly bear's claws!

How do you think harpy eagles find their prey in thick forests?

talons

grizzly bear claws

8

Harpy eagles are named after a creature from ancient Greek **myths**. A harpy has the head of a human and the body of an eagle.

back talon

9

Hunting Machine

When it's time to find food, a harpy eagle flies from tree to tree.

It uses its long tail feathers to help it steer.

Large eyes help the bird spot animals hiding among the leaves and branches.

The skillful **predator** may also fly below the treetops where there is less light.

Then the eagle uses its excellent sense of hearing to locate prey.

wing

tail feathers

Top Predator

Once a harpy eagle finds its prey, it grabs the animal with its sharp talons.

Harpy eagles can catch large, heavy animals such as monkeys, sloths, coatis, and porcupines.

The birds are the apex, or top, predator in their forest home.

This means they eat many of their neighbors, but nothing eats them!

coati

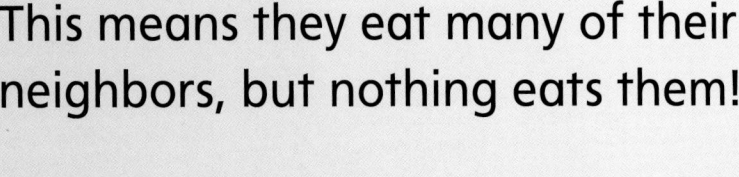

coati

porcupine

sloth

A harpy eagle uses its strong, curved beak to cut through the thick fur of a monkey or sloth. Then it uses its beak to tear off chunks of meat.

A Giant Nest

Adult harpy eagles live in pairs.

When it's time to raise a family, a male and female find a safe place in a tall tree.

Together, the eagles collect branches and build a nest.

The nest may contain more than 300 large branches.

It's big enough to fit two adult people inside!

a female eagle collecting twigs

A harpy eagle breaks branches off a tree to build its nest. The bird holds a branch in its talons, flaps its wings, and then pulls hard with its powerful feet to snap the branch.

male

female

nest

One Tiny Chick

Inside the giant nest, the female eagle lays one large white egg.

Then she sits on the egg to keep it warm.

The male eagle brings her food.

After about 55 days, a tiny chick hatches from the egg.

The baby eagle is so small it can fit in a person's hand.

eggshell

a harpy eagle chick hatching

Sometimes a female lays two eggs. The chick that hatches out of the first egg gets all of its mother's attention. As a result, the baby in the second egg usually dies.

chick

What do you think the eagle parents do once the chick has hatched?

17

Hungry Baby

The newborn chick is hungry and begs for food.

The father eagle goes hunting and brings back sloths and other prey to the nest.

The mother eagle tears off small pieces of meat and feeds them to her baby.

The chick grows quickly.

By the time the young eagle is six months old, it's the same size as its parents!

A scientist found this on the ground below a harpy eagle's nest. What do you think it is?
(The answer is on page 24.)

mother eagle

A mother harpy eagle stays in the nest with her chick until it's four months old. Then she leaves her baby for short periods of time to go hunting.

four-month-old chick

19

A Predator Grows Up

At six months old, the eagle chick is ready to leave the nest and learn to fly.

At first it crashes from branch to branch, but soon it can fly as well as the adults.

A young harpy eagle stays with its parents until it's about two years old.

Then it's ready to become the top predator of its own area of the rain forest!

A chick practices flapping its wings.

seven-month-old chick

When it's about five years old, a harpy eagle finds a partner. The birds will stay together for the rest of their lives. Harpy eagles can live for about 30 years.

How does a young harpy eagle look different from an adult? How does it look the same?

Science Lab

How Strong Is a Harpy Eagle?

An adult harpy eagle can carry prey that weighs up to 10 pounds (4.5 kg) as it flies. Let's investigate the bird's strength!

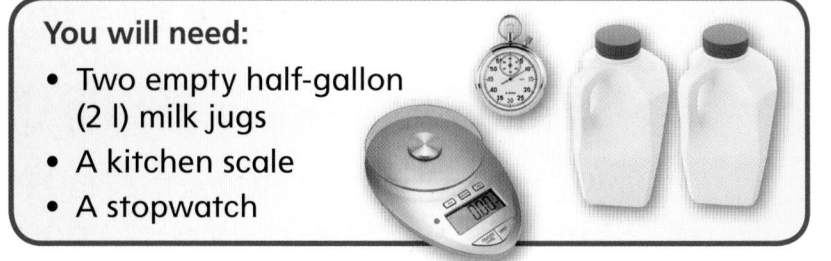

You will need:
- Two empty half-gallon (2 l) milk jugs
- A kitchen scale
- A stopwatch

1. Fill two empty milk jugs with water so they are about three-quarters full.

2. Weigh the jugs on a kitchen scale. Add or remove water until each jug weighs 5 pounds (2.3 kg).

3. Hold a jug in each hand. Now walk around your home or school for about one minute.

- *Did you find it difficult or easy to carry this amount of weight?*

- *What difficulties do you think an eagle might have carrying this weight?*

(The answers are on page 24.)

a harpy eagle with prey

Science Words

myths (MITHS) traditional stories that often tell of mysterious beings or events

predator (PRED-uh-tur) an animal that hunts other animals for food

prey (PRAY) an animal that is hunted and eaten by another animal

rain forest (RAYN FOR-ist) a large area of land covered with trees and other plants where lots of rain falls

raptors (RAP-terz) birds of prey, such as eagles and hawks

talons (TAL-uhnz) the sharp claws of a bird of prey

Index

Read More

Gagne, Tammy. *Eagles (Built for the Hunt).* North Mankato, MN: Capstone (2016).

Haywood, Karen. *Eagles (Endangered!).* New York: Cavendish Square (2008).

Jennings, Rosemary. *Eagles (Raptors!).* New York: Rosen (2016).

Learn More Online

To learn more about harpy eagles, visit
www.bearportpublishing.com/ApexPredators

About the Author

Ellen Lawrence lives in the United Kingdom. Her favorite books to write are those about nature and animals. In fact, the first book Ellen bought for herself when she was six years old was the story of a gorilla named Patty Cake that was born in New York's Central Park Zoo.

Answers

Page 18: A harpy eagle may eat an animal's fur, bones, and claws. Its body cannot break down these things, so the eagle spits them back up in a lump called a pellet. This pellet contains the fur and claws of a sloth!

Page 22: When a harpy eagle is carrying a 10-pound (4.5 kg) animal, it may have to fly a long distance and move between tangled branches. Also, if the prey isn't already dead, it may be wriggling and trying to escape from the eagle's talons. This makes it difficult for the bird to carry its meal, too.